SCHOLASTIC SCIENCE™

LEVEL
1
AGES 5 AND 6

BATS

Lily Wood

SCHOLASTIC
REFERENCE

PHOTO CREDITS: Cover: Hans Christoph Kappel/British Broadcasting Corporation Natural History Unit
Page 1: Robert & Linda Mitchell; 3: Merlin D. Tuttle/Bat Conservation International; 4: Merlin D. Tuttle/BCI/Photo Researchers; 5: Skip Moody/Dembinsky Photo Associates; 6: Dave Roberts/Photo Researchers; 7: Merlin D. Tuttle/BCI; 8: Robert & Linda Mitchell; 9: Robert & Linda Mitchell; 10-11: Dietmar Nill/BBC Natural History Unit; 12-13: Robert & Linda Mitchell; 15: Jay Ireland & Georgienne E. Bradley; 16: Dietmar Nill/BBC Natural History Unit; 17: Robert & Linda Mitchell; 18-19: Merlin D. Tuttle/BCI; 20-21: Merlin D. Tuttle/BCI; 22: Rob & Ann Simpson; 25: Merlin D. Tuttle/BCI; 26: Merlin D. Tuttle/BCI; 29: Organization for Bat Conservation; 30: Stephen Krasemann/Tony Stone Images.

ISBN 0-439-16293-9

Book design by Barbara Balch and Kay Petronio

10 9 8 7 6 5 4 3 2   01 02 03

Printed in the U.S.A.   23

First printing, October 2000

We are grateful to Francie Alexander, reading specialist, and to Adele M. Brodkin, Ph.D., developmental psychologist, for their contributions to the development of this series.

Our thanks also to our science consultant Kim Williams, executive director of the Organization for Bat Conservation.

Have you seen bats?
Most bats fly at night. Look at
the sky. Look for dark wings.

Bats turn fast. They flap
their wings. They catch bugs
in the air.

Close-up of a bat's fur

Bats fly. But bats are not birds. Birds have feathers. Bats do not. Bats have fur.

Bats' wings are not the same as birds' wings.

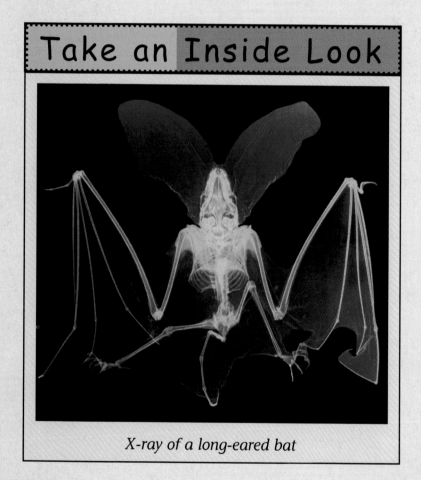

Take an Inside Look

X-ray of a long-eared bat

There are many kinds of
bats. Some bats can climb,
hop, or swim. But bats fly
most of the time.

Bats are **mammals**. Mother mammals feed milk to their babies. Bats are the only mammals that fly.

Bats sleep upside down. Bats have claws that cling to trees and cave walls.

Take a Closer Look

Close-up of a bat's claws

Bats live in many parts of
the world. Bats can live in
caves.

Bats can live inside trees.
Bats can live in attics. Bats
can live under bridges.

Some bats live in small families.
Some bats live in large groups.

Large or small, these groups
are called **colonies**.

Most bats eat bugs or fruit. Some bats drink the sweet juice inside flowers.

Vampire bats bite cows and birds. They lick a tiny bit of blood. Blood is their food.

Bats fly at night. They use sound to find their way.

A bat makes sounds through its mouth or nose.

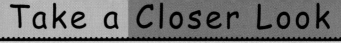

Close-up of a bat's ears

These sounds bounce off objects. The sound comes back to the bat's ears as an echo. This helps the bat locate an object.

17

Bats use echoes to find things. This is called **echolocation** (ek-oh-loh-**kay**-shuhn).

Bats use echolocation to
find and catch bugs at night.

In winter some bats
migrate (**mye**-grate).

These bats travel to warmer places for the winter.

21

Other bats **hibernate** (**hye**-bur-nate). They spend the winter in a cave, a building, or a tree.

When a bat hibernates, its heartbeat and breathing slow down.

Each year a mother bat usually has one **pup**. A pup is a baby bat.

While the mother bat hunts for food, the pup stays home.

When the mother returns, she finds the pup by its call and its smell. She can always find her pup.

Bats help farmers. They eat bugs that munch on farmers' crops.

Like bees, bats carry pollen from plant to plant. This helps plants make seeds.

Today it is hard for bats to find homes. Many trees have been cut down.

Some people help bats. People put up bat houses in their yards. These are new homes for bats.

Click, click, the bats call. The bats fly out of houses. The bats fly out of caves. The bats fly up into the sky.

Glossary

colonies—groups of animals, such as bats, that live together in the same place

echolocation (ek-oh-loh-**kay**-shuhn)—to find (locate) objects by sending out sounds, then listening to the sound that bounces back (the echo)

hibernate (**hye**-bur-nate)—to enter a sleeplike state in winter

mammals—animals that feed milk to their babies

migrate (**mye**-grate)—to take a seasonal journey from one place to another

pup—a baby bat

A Note to Parents

Learning to read is such an exciting time in a child's life. You may delight in sharing your favorite fairy tales and picture books with your child.

But don't forget the importance of introducing your child to the world of nonfiction. The ability to read and comprehend factual material will be essential to your child in school, and throughout life. The Scholastic Science Readers™ series was created especially with beginning readers in mind. These books, with their clear texts and beautiful photographs, will help you to introduce *your* new reader to the wonders of science.

Suggested Activity

To see large numbers of wild bats, you can visit the Congress Avenue Bridge in Austin, Texas. Celebrate bats at Carlsbad Caverns National Park in Carlsbad, New Mexico, which hosts an annual International Bat Festival. But you may not even need to travel to "go batty." Local zoos, children's museums, and parks often have bat exhibits or sponsor bat-related activities.